# Taxation by Telecommunications Regulation

# Taxation by Telecommunications Regulation

## The Economics of the E-Rate

Jerry Hausman

The AEI Press

Publisher for the American Enterprise Institute

WASHINGTON, D.C.

1998

*Alex Brill, Susan Dynarski, and Hyde Hsu provided research assistance. Jim Poterba and Tim Tardiff provided helpful comments.*

Distributed to the Trade by National Book Network, 15200 NBN Way, Blue Ridge Summit, PA 17214. To order call toll free 1-800-462-6420 or 1-717-794-3800. For all other inquiries please contact the AEI Press, 1150 Seventeenth Street, N.W., Washington, D.C. 20036 or call 1-800-862-5801.

ISBN 0-8447-7121-X

1 3 5 7 9 10 8 6 4 2

THE AEI PRESS
Publisher for the American Enterprise Institute
1150 17th Street, N.W., Washington, D.C. 20036

*Printed in the United States of America*

# Contents

# Foreword

Regulated industries such as telecommunications, transportation, and electric power have always had numerous "cross-subsidies" embedded in their rate structures. To promote "universal service" or just to satisfy the demands of politically influential consumer groups, state and federal regulatory agencies have set rates for some services at levels below the costs of supplying them and other rates at levels commensurately higher than costs of supply. As a result, some consumers have paid what amounts to a tax on their telephone and electricity bills to finance subsidized service to other consumers. The pattern of cross-subsidies has generally been from business customers to residential customers and from urban to rural customers—but the subsidies have often been highly complex as well as oblique, with numerous exceptions, anomalies, and departures from the general pattern built into regulated rate structures.

This "taxation by regulation" has drawn heavy criticism from academic students of regulation. Political scientists have noted that it is a form of public finance operating outside the usual legislative and executive procedures of taxing, appropriation, and budgeting—procedures that promote political accountability and restrain the influence of narrow interest groups in most areas of government spending. Economists have noted that cross-subsidies are usually highly inefficient: taxing customers of a particular service (say, business users of long-distance telephone service) to fund subsidized service to others produces far greater economic distortions than if a broad-based general tax funded the subsidized service.

The academic criticisms have had very little influence on practical policy; indeed, they have provided a powerful explanation of why cross-subsidies are so pervasive despite being so wasteful. Precisely because the source of tax revenues is obscure and "stealthy"—invisibly embedded in the prices large numbers of utility customers pay—taxation by regulation is an attractive means of subsidizing politically influential groups—including some customers, such as the well-to-do who own vacation homes in the country, who would be unlikely candidates for public largess if the subsidies were a matter of open legislative debate.

In recent years, however, cross-subsidization has come under pressure from a different, more powerful source: technological and economic developments that have generated new entry and price and service rivalry in regulated markets, thereby undermining the private monopolies and public regulation that had been the source of the cross-subsidies. In the typical case, new competition has first emerged in the "taxed" segments of the regulated rate structure, such as urban and business telephone service and industrial electric power, which have presented attractive targets for new entrants precisely because of their artificially high rates. Price competition, with its usual result of compressing prices to costs of supply, has obliged regulators and legislators to search for other revenue sources—such as other regulated services where competitive entry remains difficult—to fund continued below-cost service to favored customers. Where industries have been completely deregulated, legislators have occasionally turned to explicit general taxes to continue subsidizing those who had benefited from cross-subsidies. The Airline Deregulation Act of 1979, for example, which entirely abolished federal and state regulation of airline fares, established a grant program for "essential air service" to certain rural communities that is funded by general tax revenues.

The Telecommunications Act of 1996 provides an important case study in the tensions between deregulation and "universal service" subsidies. The Telecommunications Act did not go nearly so far as the Airline Deregulation Act in lifting government controls from an increasingly competitive industry. It did, however, relax or remove several of those controls, including price controls that had long been employed to "tax" many telecommunications services. At the same time, the act instructed the Federal Communications Commission to continue promoting universal service—but *without* access to explicit federal tax revenues such as those provided by the Airline Deregulation Act.

How, if at all, this circle might be squared is the subject of the present study by Jerry Hausman of the Massachusetts Institute of Technology. Using economic techniques he pioneered in other contexts, Professor Hausman examines one of the FCC's most striking and controversial "universal service" policies under the Telecommunications Act of 1996. This is the so-called e-rate program, under which certain schools and libraries are receiving subsidized computer facilities, Internet hookups, and telecommunications services funded by a special charge on the long-distance revenues of AT&T, MCI, Sprint, and other suppliers of long-distance and wireless services.

As one would predict, the commission's e-rate scheme abandons the old and now infeasible technique of embedding subsidies within the rate structure and instead makes the taxes and subsidies explicit. Long-distance carriers, and through them their customers, are taxed the costs of the program, and the commission pays out the tax revenues in cash grants to qualifying schools and libraries. More surprising, perhaps, is that the commission is using the new subsidies not just to maintain but to expand— quite substantially—traditional regulatory cross-subsidies. No one received free or cut-rate computers when FCC rate regulation was in full flower; now, however, schools and libraries will spend a large share of e-rate grants (which analysts project will total several billion dollars annually) to purchase sophisticated computers and to build or refurbish facilities to accommodate them. Yet one critical element of the traditional cross-subsidy approach remains: the program's revenue source is a usage-sensitive tax on certain regulated services. The commission selected that source, of course, not out of considerations of economic efficiency, political fairness, or legislative logrolling, but simply because the taxed service falls within its regulatory jurisdiction. The FCC appears to be transforming itself from an architect of cross-subsidies and promoter of universal service *within* telecommunications markets to a tax collector for funds to subsidize *other* markets and purposes.

The e-rate program has been the subject of lively and sometimes heated controversy since the commission first imposed the e-rate taxes at the beginning of 1998. Advocates say that the program is essential to ensure that poor communities and schoolchildren are not left behind on the "information highway." Opponents say that schools that cannot teach their students to read and write should not be plugging them into the Internet instead—and that Washington should not, in any event, be determining school and library spending priorities. Some say that the program, regardless of its merits, is unconstitutional because it establishes, calibrates, and collects taxes—functions the Constitution vests in Congress.

Professor Hausman's study focuses on a separate and more analytically tractable issue, but one that has important implications for the broader political debates. He asks whether the e-rate tax is an efficient tax, in the sense of raising a sum of public revenue with minimum disruption to private economic activity. He finds that the tax is appallingly inefficient, causing more than one dollar of sheer waste—deadweight economic costs that produce no benefits for anyone—for every dollar of revenue raised.

Tax distortions of that magnitude are exceptionally high compared with broad-based general taxes and even with the implicit taxes embodied in traditional regulatory cross-subsidies. The result leads Professor Hausman to ask whether the FCC has actually *maximized*, rather than minimized, the cost to economic welfare of its e-rate program and to suggest several alternatives that, even without resort to general federal tax revenues, would be far less harmful.

Congress intended the Telecommunications Act of 1996 to reduce regulatory costs and improve consumer welfare in one of America's most rapidly growing and socially important industries. Professor Hausman's study demonstrates that one critical component of that act is instead increasing regulatory costs and harming consumer welfare. No one ever said that the transition from regulated to competitive markets would be easy or free of political controversy, compromise, and false steps—but the e-rate tax appears to be a step backward rather than a partial step forward. One hopes that the FCC and Congress, as well as business executives, professionals, and academics will pay due attention to this cautionary tale.


CHRISTOPHER DEMUTH
President
American Enterprise Institute
for Public Policy Research

HAROLD FURCHTGOTT-ROTH
Commissioner
Federal Communications Commission

# 1
# Introduction

Policy makers have paid increasing attention to telecommunications as new features such as cellular
telephones and Internet services have become
widely available to businesses and consumers. Rapidly
changing technology has led to these new services along
with the realization that market-based competition may
replace much outdated regulation, which has harmed consumers (see, for example, Hausman 1997). Congress passed
the Telecommunications Act of 1996, the first major change
in telecommunications legislation since 1934, in response
to these changes.

What role does public finance have in the analysis of
telecommunications policy? Telecommunications regulation in the United States is replete with a system of subsidies and taxes, in part because of the dual system of
regulation in which the federal government (through the
Federal Communications Commission) and each state have
regulatory jurisdiction over local telephone companies.[1]
Public finance analysis demonstrates how to evaluate the
costs and benefits of tax and subsidy systems.[2] Indeed,
public finance analysis demonstrates how to measure the
distortions to economic efficiency that tax and subsidy
systems create.[3] Furthermore, public finance analysis has
determined rules for optimal taxation that can be applied
to telecommunications regulation.[4]

A potentially important application of public finance analysis to telecommunications regulation is the financing by regulation of telephone companies' fixed and common costs. The technological characteristics of the local telecommunications industry with its large fixed costs generate significant economies of scale and scope. The first-best prescription of setting price equal to marginal cost would require government subsidies or would lead to bankruptcy of local telephone companies.[5] The United States has not used government subsidies; instead, regulators have set price in excess of marginal cost for some services to allow regulated telephone companies to cover their fixed and common costs and to provide a subsidy to basic residential service. Here Ramsey optimal tax theory, which explains how taxes on different goods or services cause different amounts of economic efficiency loss depending on the elasticity of demand for the good or service being taxed, would suggest how prices should exceed marginal costs to minimize the efficiency losses to the economy.[6] While Ramsey theory was devised for the purpose of raising revenue in just the situation that regulators face, it has found little acceptance in telephone regulation, perhaps because most of the tax burden would fall on local telephone service, which actually receives the highest subsidy of any telephone service. Estimates of the different relevant elasticities of demand necessary for Ramsey theory to be applied appear later in this discussion.

Another potential application for public finance analysis in telecommunications regulation, and the main topic of this volume, is the marginal cost to the economy of the new congressional legislation that leads to additional taxation of telecommunications services. Because of budgetary spending limits, Congress is increasingly unable to raise general taxes to pay for social programs.[7] Thus, Congress increasingly funds social programs from taxes on specific sectors of the economy. Here, I consider the congressional legislation that established a program to provide subsidized Internet services to all schools and libraries in the United States. The cost of the program is currently estimated to reach $2.25 billion per year in 2007.[8] Instead of increasing general taxes to fund this program, Congress passed legislation that directed all interstate telephone service providers to pay for the program. Congress let the FCC determine the appropriate rate of the new subsidy.[9]

In this volume, I calculate the efficiency cost to the economy of the increased taxation of interstate telephone services to fund the Internet access discounts to schools and libraries.[10] I do not attempt to measure the benefits, but for reasoned policy decisions the cost estimates are useful.[11] I estimate the cost to the economy of raising the $2.25 billion per year to be at least $2.36 billion (in addition to the $2.25 billion of tax revenue) or the efficiency loss to the economy for every $1 raised to pay for the Internet access discounts is an additional $1.05 to $1.25 beyond the money raised for the discounts themselves.[12] This cost to the economy is extraordinarily high compared with other taxes used by the federal government to raise revenues. Three reasons exist for the high cost to the economy of this increased tax on interstate long-distance services: (1) the price elasticity of long-distance services is relatively high; (2) the taxation of interstate long-distance services is already quite high; and (3) the price-to-marginal-cost ratio of long-distance services is high. Thus, the FCC's choice of a tax instrument to finance the Internet discounts imposes extremely high efficiency costs on the U.S. economy.

Next, I propose an alternative method by which the FCC could have raised the revenue for the Internet discounts that would have a near zero cost to the economy, beyond the revenues raised. Econometric research has led to wide agreement on the relative size of telephone service price elasticities, and the FCC could have chosen to increase taxes already in place, which would have led to much lower costs to the economy of funding the Internet discounts. Indeed, economic theory and public finance analysis establish the goal of using taxes that *minimize* the cost to the economy of raising government revenue. The FCC, to the contrary, chose the taxation method applied to interstate telephone service that likely *maximizes* the cost to the economy of raising the revenue to provide the Internet discounts.

Taxpayers can hope that the FCC will begin to take heed of economic analysis in the future as it continues to modify the tax and subsidy system for telecommunications. The Telecommunications Act of 1996 calls for further modifications to regulation in the future. Telecommunications regulation at the federal level has always recognized the "public interest standard" as one of the main bases for regulation. The public interest standard should recognize economic efficiency as one of its primary goals. Economic efficiency implies not assessing unnecessary costs on U.S. consumers and firms. The FCC's current policies are costing the U.S. economy billions or tens of billions of dollars per year. The goal of the Telecommunications Act of 1996 was to decrease these regulatory costs to the United States, not to increase them as the FCC has done in its implementation of provisions of the 1996 act.

# 2
# Regulation of U.S. Telecommunications

Regulation of telecommunications in the United States is unique among all countries in that two levels of government regulate telephone service: the federal government through the FCC and each of fifty-one state (including the District of Columbia) regulatory commissions. In broad principle, the FCC is in charge of interstate telecommunications, while the state regulatory commissions are in charge of intrastate telecommunications. Although the FCC has periodically attempted to make "power grabs" to attain more control over regulation, the state commissions have resisted those attempts. In two notable decisions, the *Louisiana* decision (1986) and recently in the interconnection decision by the Eighth Circuit Court of Appeals in July 1997, [13] the courts have upheld the states. Both times, the appeals courts have narrowly circumscribed the ability of the FCC to intervene in intrastate telecommunications regulation.

As most users of a telephone realize, however, the same telephone wire that connects a residence to the local central office switch, the switch itself, and the fiber-optic cable that connects the switch to other switches carry both intrastate calls and interstate calls. Thus, no natural boundary exists to demarcate spheres of regulation.

During the years in which regulators used cost-based or rate-of-return regulation, they arbitrarily separated the rate base into an intrastate portion and an interstate portion, based primarily on the relative number of calls of each type. The "separations" system has achieved an increasingly complicated level of detail that only a regulatory accountant could love and perhaps no living person can understand in its entirety.[14] If the system ever made sense, it has no basis in economic reality today, since both the FCC and a majority of the states no longer use rate-based regulation.

The end result of the separations system is that the FCC interstate regulation is responsible for about 25 percent of the local exchange companies' assets, and state regulators are responsible for the other 75 percent. Under rate-of-return regulation, the regulated telephone companies' profits in each regulatory regime were meant to be large enough to allow the firms to earn their regulated cost of capital on these regulatory-determined rate bases.

Before the breakup of AT&T in 1984, long-distance service cross-subsidized local residential service through intracompany transfers, the result of an earlier agreement with regulators and the Ozark Plan of 1971.[15] After the AT&T divestiture, regulators had to establish an explicit subsidy flow to continue the cross-subsidy of local residential service.[16] The FCC established a per minute of use access fee that long-distance companies had to pay local telephone companies for the use of their networks to originate and terminate long-distance calls.[17] The commission initially set access fees at quite high rates, about 17.3 cents per minute for both origination and termination. The access fees had the same effect as a tax on long-distance calls because the access fee paid for the subsidy to local residential service as well as for some of the fixed and common costs of the local exchange companies that were included in the FCC's 25 percent share of the local exchange companies' rate bases over which the FCC held jurisdiction.[18]

These access charges were not a very economically efficient set of taxes because studies funded by AT&T Bell Laboratories and other researchers have consistently demonstrated an interstate long-distance price elasticity of about −0.7.[19] Furthermore, policy makers did not seriously analyze the fundamental question of whether every residential telephone customer should receive a cross-subsidy, no matter what his income. Policy makers discussed cross-subsidies of local telephone service under the rubric of "universal service," which was part of the Communications Act of 1934. By 1984, however, telephone penetration in the United States was about 91.5 percent, with additional targeted subsidies in place for low-income customers. In Washington, D.C., for example, Bell Atlantic offers local phone service to qualifying households for $3 a month and to qualifying senior citizens for only $1 a month.

Current telephone penetration is about 93.9 percent. Econometric studies that I conducted did not show any significant "network effects" at this level of penetration; I am unaware of any econometric studies that did show a significant network externality.[20] Thus, the replacement of a universal cross-subsidy with targeted subsidies (telephone stamps, for example) would have been more economically efficient than access charges for long-distance service. But policy makers never seriously considered such a rational policy.

In 1984, the FCC adopted a framework that did allow for a significant decrease in long-distance access charges. It adopted a "subscriber line charge" (SLC), which reached $3.50 per line per month for residential households and $6.00 per line per month for businesses. Access rates for long-distance sevice decreased from about 17 cents per minute to about 9.5 cents per minute (for both origination and termination), primarily as a result of the advent of the SLC. The FCC considered a higher SLC that would have decreased long-distance access rates even more, but Washington lobbying groups such as the Consumer Federation of America (CFA) made apocalyptic forecasts of 6 million households' stopping their telephone service, which would have decreased telephone penetration below 85 percent. As with much of the policy debate over telephone regulation during the past twenty years, the CFA's forecasts were based on little real economics and proved to be vastly inaccurate. Indeed, telephone penetration increased because of the SLC and lower access prices, as demonstrated by Hausman, Tardiff, and Belinfante (1993).

The SLC was quite unlikely to bring about large decreases in telephone penetration since an increase in the SLC leads directly to lower long-distance prices and telephone subscribers needed local service to make long-distance calls. Available data at that time demonstrated that low-income households made numerous long-distance calls; indeed, long-distance charges accounted for about half their monthly telephone charges. Thus, economic analysis led to the conclusions that consumers buy telephone service for both local and long-distance calls and, because an increase in the SLC would be more than counteracted by the decrease in long-distance call prices, that the monthly bill of the large majority of residential customers would decrease when the number of long-distance calls was held constant. Economic-efficiency calculations demonstrated that consumers would be made better off by billions of dollars per year if the SLC were further increased and the long-distance charges decreased. Nevertheless, the FCC refused to allow the SLC to increase further, even at the rate of inflation.

# 3
# Studies of Telephone Demand

T o determine the economically efficient method of taxation within telecommunications regulation, given that subsidies are unlikely to disappear soon, we need estimates of certain demand elasticities. First, I discuss the price elasticity of demand for interstate long-distance service. In the original edition of Taylor (1994), the author had estimated this elasticity to be about −0.7 on the basis of 1970s data. Subsequent studies based on data from the 1980s by Gatto et al. (1988), Taylor and Taylor (1993), and Taylor (1994) have continued to estimate very similar elasticities.[21] Thus, the "consensus" elasticity estimates for interstate long-distance calls are in the range of −0.65 to −0.75.[22]

The demand elasticity for local exchange access is the next important piece of information. Throughout the United States with the exception of New York City, most residential customers buy unlimited-use local calling, so-called flat-rate local service.[23] This service also allows the consumer to make long-distance calls, typically through a presubscribed long-distance carrier such as AT&T or MCI. The imposition of the SLC as well as other local rate increases in the 1980s and the decrease in long-distance prices caused mainly by the decrease in access charges

9

allow relatively precise estimation of the demand for residential service.[24]

Hausman, Tardiff, and Belinfante (1993) modeled the demand for local access as a partially indirect utility function that recognized the demand for both local calls and long-distance calls. Details of this model and its significance appear in appendix A. The study by Hausman et al. used panel data for the years 1984–1988 from a random sample of about 55,000 households. The study estimated the elasticity with respect to the basic access price to be −0.005, which is quite small, with a 10 percent price increase leading to a 0.5 percent decrease in penetration (which is approximately 0.005 given a penetration rate of about 93 percent). The finding of a very small but significantly nonzero own-price elasticity for residential basic access demand is consistent with prior studies, with the best known the paper of Perl (1984), and with subsequent studies such as those by Ericksson, Kaserman, and Mayo (1995) and Solvason (1997).

The small but negative price elasticity effect has led some regulators to resist raising basic access prices because of the negative effect it would have on telephone penetration. Concentration only on the own-price effect, however, could lead to incorrect conclusions. Hausman, Tardiff, and Belinfante (1993) estimated that the cross-price elasticity of the demand for basic access service with respect to the price of calls within a local access and transport area (intraLATA)[25] is −0.0086. Cross-price elasticity with respect to interstate toll service is −0.0055, almost as high. This demonstrates the complementary nature of basic access demand and local and long-distance telephone usage. As prices for local access increase, demand for long-distance service decreases. But an *increase* in basic access price combined with a *decrease* in long-distance toll prices (through a decrease in long-distance access prices) could well lead to an *increase* rather than a decrease in telephone penetration. Hausman et al. concluded that the imposition of the SLC and the associated decrease in long-distance prices led to an *increase* in telephone penetration of about 450,000 households. Thus, the SLC had led to increased telephone penetration and increased economic efficiency since the lower access fees led to lower distance prices, which led to a significant increase in long-distance calls.

# 4
# Estimation of Economic Efficiency Losses

axes (and subsidies) distort economic activity. Taxes
increase prices and thus lead to lower demand. This
lower demand has two adverse effects on economic
efficiency, which is defined (approximately) as the sum of
producer surplus and consumer surplus.[26] To the extent
that the industry is imperfectly competitive and price exceeds marginal cost to cover fixed costs, decreased demand
reduces the amount of producer surplus, which is the product of quantity demanded times the difference between
price and marginal cost.[27] Decreased demand from higher
prices also affects consumers adversely since consumer
surplus decreases. Thus, the change in economic efficiency
from the imposition of a tax is given approximately by

$$\Delta E \approx \Delta q(p-mc) + 0.5\Delta q\Delta p, \qquad (4\text{--}1)$$

where the first term on the right side is the change in
producer surplus and the second term is the change in
consumer surplus, after I subtract the amount raised by
the tax.[28] Figure 4–1 graphs this relationship.

A more accurate method than equation (4–1) replaces
the second term on the right side of equation (4–1) with a
calculation of the exact deadweight loss to consumers on

## FIGURE 4–1
### EFFICIENCY LOSS CAUSED BY TAXATION

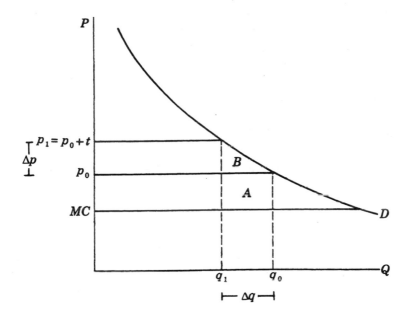

SOURCE: Author.

the basis of the analysis of Hausman (1981a). An explanation of this technique appears in appendix B.

## Calculation of the Losses

Using equation (4–1), the long-distance elasticity estimate considered above, and the fact that the marginal cost of long-distance service is at most about 25 percent of the price while the long-distance access rate is \$0.0604 per minute, I estimate that for average revenue raised by the tax on long-distance service, the change in efficiency is $(0.654)*(TR)$, where $TR$ is tax revenue raised. The first term on the right side of equation (4–1) (after dividing by tax revenue $TR$) is estimated to be 0.415, and the second term is estimated to be 0.239. Thus, the average efficiency loss to the economy for each $1 raised through the access tax is $0.65, which is quite high, as we shall subsequently see. Indeed, by changing the method by which policy makers raise the access "tax" revenue, they could reduce this efficiency loss to essentially zero (see Hausman 1995).

Using the exact approach based on Hausman (1981a), I calculate the average efficiency loss to the economy for each $1 raised through the access tax to be $0.79 instead of the $0.65 that I estimated by using the traditional approximation based on equation (4–1). Thus, I find that the exact calculation leads to a higher estimate of average efficiency loss than the approximate method based on a Taylor expansion.

Perhaps a more relevant calculation is the marginal efficiency loss to the economy, since the access tax is already in place and the recent FCC action to fund the Internet subsidy to schools and libraries increased the tax (or at least caused it not to decrease as much as it would have). The formula for the marginal efficiency loss appears in appendix C and is calculated to be 1.249. Thus, the marginal efficiency loss is extremely high, since for each dollar raised by an increase in the access tax, $1.25 of efficiency loss is created for the economy, beyond the tax revenue raised. Using $1.89 billion of the $2.25 billion of revenue per year for the Internet subsidy leads to an estimate of the efficiency loss to the U.S. economy of $2.36 billion per year.[29]

When I calculate the marginal efficiency loss by using the exact calculation based on Hausman (1981a) instead of the traditional approximation, I estimate the marginal efficiency loss to be $1.250, which is almost exactly the same as the previous estimate of $1.249.[30] Thus, for the marginal efficiency loss calculation the two methods lead to virtually identical results.

Three reasons exist for this high marginal efficiency loss to the economy: (1) the elasticity $\eta_i$ is relatively high;

TABLE 4-1
MARGINAL EFFICIENCY EFFECTS OF ADDITIONAL TAXES RAISED

| Study | Type of Taxes | Marginal Effect (dollars) |
|---|---|---|
| 1. Ballard, Shoven, and Whalley (1985) | U.S. taxes | 0.365 |
| 2. Browning (1987) | U.S. taxes | 0.395 |
| 3. Bovenberg and Goulder (1996) | U.S. taxes | 0.260 |
| 4. Hausman (1981b) | Income taxes | 0.405 |

NOTE: Where a range of estimates is given in the original paper, I use the midpoint of the range. Feldstein (1995) has estimated significantly higher marginal efficiency losses from the income tax.

(2) $m_i/p_i$ is relatively low since gross margins are high in long-distance service, which is to be expected given the large fixed costs of telecommunications networks; and (3) $t_i/p_i$ is high since a significant proportion of the subsidy to local service and contribution to the network's fixed and common costs comes from access charges on interstate long-distance service. To see how this efficiency loss compares with other taxes in the U.S. economy, I turn to a review of the literature.

**Previous Estimates**

Instead of taxing the use of telecommunications services to fund the subsidy for Internet access for schools and libraries, Congress could have used general tax revenue. While no generally agreed-to number exists for the value of the marginal efficiency loss to the economy from increasing total taxes, the range of estimates is reasonably close. In table 4-1, I present estimates of marginal effects of additional taxes.

All the estimates in table 4-1 are below $0.405 of

marginal efficiency loss per dollar of additional revenue raised. Thus, they are all less than one-third of the efficiency loss created by the FCC when it increased the access rates on interstate long-distance service to fund the Internet subsidy. Congress and the FCC have used an extraordinarily expensive means to fund that subsidy.[31]

# 5
# Did the FCC Maximize the Efficiency Loss?

Given that taxes create economic distortions and lead to losses in producer surplus and consumer surplus, economic analysis suggests that policy makers should choose taxes to minimize the efficiency-loss effect on the economy.[32] I believe that the FCC chose the tax to fund the Internet subsidy, however, by the method that likely *maximizes* the loss in economic efficiency. Even if the tax chosen by the FCC did not absolutely maximize efficiency loss, it imposed extremely high and unnecessary efficiency costs on the economy. I first demonstrate an alternative method to raise the revenue for the Internet subsidy that leads to almost zero (or even negative) loss in economic efficiency and then discuss the policy options of the FCC.

## The Effect of Increasing the Subscriber Line Charge

As an alternative method, the FCC could have raised the revenue for the Internet subsidy by increasing the subscriber line charge. The FCC has not increased the SLC for residential households since 1984, despite about 58.6 percent inflation since that time. The SLC largely funds the joint and common costs of the local exchange carriers' networks as well as the cross-subsidy for local exchange access (for example, local telephone service). Note that in its efficiency effects on the economy, the SLC is very attractive. Hausman, Tardiff, and Belinfante (1993) estimated the own-price elasticity of local access with respect to its price, $\eta_i$ , to be −0.005, which means that the quantity change, $\Delta q$, will be very close to zero.[33] Thus, the SLC acts like a lump-sum tax with "first-best" economic efficiency properties, since it does not create an economic distortion; that is, equation (4–1) is approximately equal to zero since $\eta_i$ is very near zero.

The FCC would have needed to increase the SLC by approximately $1.50 per month to fund the Internet subsidy of $2.25 billion per year. Note that this increase of $1.50 is $0.56 less than the amount of the inflation increase over the period 1984–1997, so that the increase would not even have returned the SLC to its original value in real terms.[34] Since Social Security and most other federal benefit programs for the needy are indexed, no increased hardship would have been created.[35]

I calculate the marginal change in economic efficiency for an additional dollar of revenue raised to be 0.0006 or an efficiency loss of about $0.0006 for each $1.00 increase in the SLC. Thus, an increase in the SLC to fund the Internet subsidy has an extremely small efficiency effect, essentially equal to zero. The calculation is detailed in appendix D and is similar to that used to measure the marginal efficiency loss from the tax on long-distance service.

### Estimated Effects of Increasing the SLC

The FCC's stated rationale for increasing long-distance access charges to fund the Internet subsidy, rather than increasing the SLC, was that telephone penetration might decrease if the SLC were increased (First Report and Order in the Matter of Access Charge Reform, FCC 97–158,

May 7, 1997, para. 55). If we use the own-price elasticity of −0.005 for local access, the estimated decrease in penetration would be about −0.04 percent, or about 39,300 households. Even if the FCC is correct about decreased telephone penetration, its policy choice led to a loss in economic efficiency of $2.36 billion per year or $60,050 per year for each household that would have stopped subscribing to telephone service. Thus, the FCC policy choice led to an extremely expensive method to fund universal service.[36] Expenditure of more than $60,000 per year per household to fund universal service could well raise questions about the policy choice.

It is not at all clear, however, that the 39,300 households would have stopped subscribing to local service. As Hausman, Tardiff, and Belinfante (1993) discuss, households subscribe to telephone service to make both local and long-distance calls. Thus, an increase in the SLC, rather than an increase in long-distance access rate that leads to an increase in long-distance prices, can have a smaller effect or even a positive effect on telephone penetration. Here, long-distance access prices would have decreased because of the price-cap system used for regulation, and long-distance prices might also have decreased.[37] The decrease in long-distance prices could well have more than offset the increase in local access prices caused by the increase in the SLC. Hausman et al. discuss how telephone penetration increased from 1984 to 1990 despite the inception of the $3.50 payment increase in the SLC and other increases in local access rates because of the decrease in long-distance prices. We calculate an increase in telephone penetration of 0.45 percent due to the inception of the SLC because the positive long-distance effect exceeded the negative SLC effect.[38] In the current situation, I cannot estimate the general effect on telephone penetration because the oligopoly interaction of the long-distance companies does not permit an estimate of the expected decrease in long-distance prices. Nevertheless, the FCC's reasoning on the effect of telephone penetration from an increase in the SLC is unlikely to be correct.

## Other Possible Policy Choices

Given that the efficiency loss to the U.S. economy of raising $1.89 billion per year by increasing the long-distance access tax is $2.36 billion, are other possible policy options available to the FCC if it does not want to increase the SLC? One option would be to use a portion of the revenues that the FCC raises each year by auctioning off spectrum. In 1995 and 1996, the FCC auctioned 120 MHz of spectrum to personal communications service providers, who use digital cellular technology. Auction revenues exceeded $10 billion. The FCC also auctioned spectrum for specialized mobile radio and has plans to auction at least another 120 MHz in the next three years. The FCC could use a portion of these revenues to fund the Internet subsidy. Doing so would create no adverse economic-efficiency effects since the revenues bid are a form of pure profits tax levied on the buyers of the spectrum.[39] Thus, use of government spectrum revenues to fund the Internet subsidy would have much lower efficiency costs to the U.S. economy than the FCC's chosen policy.

Another possible way to fund the Internet subsidy is to charge Internet users the marginal cost of using the telephone network. During peak periods, the marginal cost of Internet usage to the local telephone network is approximately $0.004–$0.008 per minute, while during offpeak periods the marginal cost is near zero. Currently, residential users of the Internet obtain local service as part of their monthly charge for Internet service. Because of long holding periods of Internet usage on a telephone network designed for short voice calls, Internet usage has created service problems in a number of areas. Setting the price of Internet access equal to its marginal cost would decrease the distortions created by the current subsidy.[40] It is unclear, however, how much revenue a fee based on marginal cost would generate, and it might be significantly less than $2.25 billion per year.

Neither of these policies would create a loss of economic efficiency. Indeed, charging Internet users their marginal cost could actually increase economic efficiency. Similarly, increasing the SLC by approximately $1.50 per month would lead to, at most, an extremely small loss in economic efficiency and could well lead to a gain in economic efficiency.

# 6
# Conclusions

The FCC controls one of the most important and dynamic industries in the U.S. economy. Many FCC policy choices, though, have been made without regard to economic considerations. For instance, in my previous research I have demonstrated that FCC policy with respect to cellular telephones cost consumers and the economy over $100 billion. Current FCC policy toward long-distance competition is likely costing consumers about $7 billion per year. These large amounts of consumer harm are significant, even in relation to efficiency considerations raised by general U.S. tax policy.

In this analysis, I consider the efficiency effect of the recent FCC policy to raise $2.25 billion per year to fund an Internet subsidy to schools and libraries. I estimate that the efficiency loss is about $1.25 per dollar raised, or a total of $2.36 billion per year on the $1.89 billion per year raised through the increase in the long-distance access tax. The FCC could have raised this same amount of revenue with little or no loss in economic efficiency by increasing the subscriber line charge. The increase in the SLC would have returned it to its initial real value when the SLC was imposed in 1984. FCC policy here had the opposite effect: the FCC chose the policy that likely maximizes the efficiency loss to the economy, instead of minimizing the efficiency loss. Since regulation of the telecommunications network in the United States is a grab bag of taxes and subsidies, the FCC needs to begin to pay attention to the efficiency effects of its regulatory policy. Otherwise, consumers and the economy will continue to lose billions of dollars per year because of regulatory policy that creates quite large inefficiencies.

APPENDIX A

# Partially Indirect Utility Function

The demand for local access model used in Hausman, Tardiff, and Belinfante (1993) is a partially indirect utility function. The function takes the form:

$$u = u\,(y,p,q,z,\varepsilon),\qquad\text{(A–1)}$$

where $y$ is household income, $p$ is a vector of prices for basic exchange access that includes the one-time installation price and the monthly basic exchange price, $q$ is a vector of prices of use of local service (whose price is often zero) and both intrastate and interstate long-distance services, $z$ is a function of household characteristics, and $\varepsilon$ is a random parameter independently distributed across households. Hausman et al. estimated the basic exchange access discrete-choice equation, in which a consumer decides whether to purchase telephone service, if

$$\tilde{u}_1 = \tilde{u}\,(y - p_1 - p_2,\, q,\, z,\, \varepsilon) \ge \tilde{u}\,(y,\, z,\, \varepsilon) = \tilde{u}_2,\qquad\text{(A–2)}$$

where $\tilde{u}_1$ is the partially indirect utility function where the basic access price has been subtracted from household income and $\tilde{u}_2$ is the partially indirect utility function where all consumption is of the composite (nontelephone) commodity. An important finding of equations (A–1) and (A–2) is that the discrete-choice equation should depend on the basic access price(s) and also the usage prices, including long-distance prices. The econometric specification is in marked contrast to almost all other previous specifications of basic access demand, which did not include long-distance prices. This specification, where the demand for local access depends on *both* the price of local access and the prices for long-distance calls, has been incorporated in subsequent studies of demand for basic access.

APPENDIX B

# Exact Calculation
# of Deadweight Loss

Instead of using the Taylor expansion, I use the expenditure function based on the log-linear demand curve to calculate the compensating variation from the increase in taxes:

$$CV = \left\{ \frac{(1-\delta)}{(1+\alpha)} y^{-\delta} [p_1 x_1 - p_0 x_0] + y^{(1-\delta)} \right\}^{1/(1-\delta)} - y, \quad \text{(B-1)}$$

where $\delta$ is the income elasticity (0.8) and $\alpha$ is the price elasticity. To calculate the deadweight loss ($DWL$) to consumers, I subtract the compensated revenue raised $R^*$ from the compensating variation calculated in equation (B-1): $DWL = CV - R^*$. The $DWL$ estimate replaces the second term on the right side of equation (4-1). Hausman (1981a) demonstrates that this exact calculation can be considerably more accurate than the approximation contained in equation (4-1).

# Marginal Efficiency Loss from Long-Distance Access Charges

We can compute the formula for the marginal efficiency loss by taking the marginal change in equation (4–1) with respect to the tax rate, $\partial \Delta E / \partial t_i$, and dividing by the marginal change in tax revenue with respect to the tax rate, $\partial TR / \partial t_i$:

$$(\frac{\partial \Delta E / \partial t_i}{\partial TR / \partial t_i}) \approx$$

$$\frac{\eta_i \frac{(1-m_i)}{p_i} + \eta_i \frac{t_i}{p_i} + \left[\eta_i \frac{t_i m_i}{p_i^2} - 0.5\eta \frac{t_i^2}{p_i^2}\right] \frac{\partial p_i}{\partial t_i}}{1 - \eta_i \frac{t_i}{p_i} \frac{\partial p_i}{\partial t_i}}.$$

(C–1)

Using equation (C–1) together with the assumption that $\partial p_i / \partial t_i = 1$ along with the fact that $t_i / p_i = 0.403$, I estimate equation (C–1) to be 1.249.[41]

APPENDIX D

# Marginal Efficiency Loss
# from an Increase in the SLC

To calculate the efficiency effects of this increase in the
SLC, I return to equation (C–1) but now compute the marginal change in economic efficiency for a change in the
SLC:

$$
\frac{\partial \Delta E}{\partial SLC} \approx
$$

$$
\frac{\eta_j \dfrac{(1-m_j)}{p_j} + \eta_j \dfrac{t_j}{p_j} + \left[\eta_j \dfrac{t_j m_j}{p_j^2} - 0.5\eta_j \dfrac{t_j^2}{p_j^2}\right] \dfrac{\partial p_j}{\partial SLC}}{1 - \eta_j \dfrac{t_j}{p_j} \dfrac{\partial p_j}{\partial SLC}}.
$$
(D–1)

I first consider the second term in the numerator of the
right side of equation (D–1), which is the change in consumer surplus (after subtracting tax revenue raised). Since
the ratio $t_j/p_j = 0.123$ for the SLC approximately, the marginal change in consumer surplus is about 0.0006, using
the assumption that $\partial p_j / \partial SLC - 1$.[42] Thus, for each additional dollar of revenue raised, the efficiency loss is about
6/100 of a penny, that is, nearly zero, as expected.

Now the first term in the numerator has a rather
surprising outcome. Regulators price local access services
for residential customers below marginal (incremental)
cost in most states as a policy to subsidize service to rural
customers and middle-class residential customers. The
ratio of $m_j/p_j$ exceeds 1.0, and a national average is approximately 1.25. Thus, the first term equals –0.0013, so
that the sum of the initial two terms in the numerator of

equation (D–1) yields a change in economic efficiency from increasing the SLC of –0.0007, actually an *increase* in economic efficiency because the subsidy is decreased. When I estimate the last two terms in the numerator and compute the denominator, I calculate the marginal efficiency loss to be 0.0006, or an efficiency loss of about $0.0006 for each $1.00 increase in the SLC. Thus, an increase in the SLC to fund the Internet subsidy has an extremely small efficiency effect, essentially equal to zero.[43]

# Notes

1. Broadly speaking, the FCC has jurisdiction over interstate calls and about 25 percent of the capital base of local telephone companies, while state regulation has jurisdiction over intrastate calls and the remaining 75 percent of the capital base. Numerous exceptions exist on the interstate-intrastate calls, and some services have aspects of both interstate and intrastate calls.

2. Some Washington lawyers might quibble about the use of *tax* here, since the FCC is allowed to assess only *fees*, not taxes. We public finance economists, however, know a tax when we see one.

3. See, for example, Auerbach (1985).

4. For an analysis of optimal taxation, see Diamond and Mirrlees (1971); and for an application of the Diamond-Mirrlees theory to telecommunications regulation, see Hausman (1995).

5. This point has long been recognized. See, for example, Kahn (1988).

6. Ramsey theory says that taxes that cause prices to increase create losses in economic efficiency, with the size of the efficiency loss depending on the price elasticities, the magnitude of the price increase $(\Delta p_i / p_i)$, the revenue of the good or service being taxed $p_i q_i$, and the marginal cost of production, $m_i$. For recent recommendations using Ramsey theory in the context of price-cap regulation, see, for example, Laffont and Tirole (1996).

7. The 1990 Budget Enforcement Act includes a pay-as-you-go restriction to tax changes and changes in entitlement programs other than Social Security. Poterba (1997) discusses the budget experience under this act.

8. This $2.25 billion per year subsidy is only a small part of a much larger framework of universal service subsidies. While Congress passed the legislation establishing the subsidies, the FCC

determined the $2.25 billion per year amount.

9. The propensity of policy makers to tax the provision of utilities goes back more than 100 years. Supposedly, Gladstone, then chancellor of the Exchequer, asked Michael Faraday about the usefulness of electricity. Faraday responded, "Why Sir, there is every probability that you will soon be able to tax it!"

10. Thus, this volume demonstrates how to answer the question raised by Posner (1971) of the cost of subsidy programs arising from regulation.

11. The question of benefits is worthy of further study. For instance, *all* public schools (and some private schools) and all public libraries receive a subsidy for their purchase of Internet access. While the subsidy scheme is progressive, over 97 percent of schools receive at least a 40 percent discount, and more than 67 percent of schools receive at least a 50 percent discount. One might question why communities such as Weston, Massachusetts, with a 1990 median family income of $95,134 and Hillsborough, California, with a 1990 median family income of $123,625 require a subsidy, especially given the relatively large proportion of high-technology–related job holders in both towns. Given the likely outcome that these towns will not change their purchase behavior even with the subsidy, the subsidy represents a pure transfer from long-distance users to taxpayers of these communities.

12. This estimate is an approximation because the funds will be raised from all interstate telecommunications services—for example, cellular telephone, not just regular long-distance service. The FCC estimates that about 1.5 percent of end-user wireless revenues will be used in the tax. Thus, I base my estimate of the efficiency loss to the economy on the assumption that $1.89 billion will be raised through a tax on long-distance calls. I do not include the additional efficiency loss to the economy from the tax on wireless services. Given my estimate of the cellular demand price elasticity (Hausman 1997), the tax on wireless will also lead to a significant additional loss in economic efficiency. Including the efficiency loss from the tax on wireless services would increase my estimate of the efficiency loss from $2.36 billion to $2.53 billion. Moreover, taking account of general-equilibrium price effects would lead to a further increase in my estimates.

13. *Louisiana Pub. Serv. Comm'n v. FCC*, 476 U.S. 355 (1986) and *Iowa Utilities Board et al. v. FCC*, Eighth Circuit, July 18, 1997.

14. In 1947 the FCC and the National Association of Regulatory Utility Commissioners jointly created a separations manual, which established the federal-state cost allocation process for the next several decades. The separations system was based on a uni-

form system of accounts prescribed for all companies under the FCC's jurisdiction.

15. The separations process distinguishes between the traffic-sensitive and non-traffic-sensitive costs. The Ozark Plan, adopted in 1970, assigned 3.3 percent of non-traffic-sensitive costs to the interstate services for every percent of actual interstate use.

In its antitrust suit against AT&T, the Department of Justice claimed that AT&T used its local access revenues to cross-subsidize its long-distance competition with MCI. This theory was incorrect as the cross-subsidy flowed in the opposite direction as subsequent events demonstrated conclusively. Indeed, the Department of Justice recognized its mistake in a court filing in 1987.

16. By the term *cross-subsidy*, I mean setting price less than long-run incremental cost.

17. The FCC established all the taxes on long-distance service that I discuss, although Congress does exercise oversight over the FCC.

18. Many other cross-subsidies and distortions arise from state regulation, such as the subsidy to rural telephone subscribers who generally are significantly more costly to serve but who pay the same rates as urban customers when served by a common local exchange carrier.

19. See, for example, Taylor (1994). These estimated elasticities were based on times-series data that led to very precise estimation given the significant decrease in long-distance prices that occurred in the 1970s. More recent estimates also lead to very precise results. Thus, a one-standard-deviation change in the elasticity estimate would not affect the results of my calculations by a significant amount. A quite interesting finding is that the price elasticity for long-distance service did not change and remained at much the same value up through the 1990s, as I discuss later. Thus, the onset of long-distance competition did not affect the price elasticity; nor did competition significantly affect the position of the demand curve over time (no outward shift of the demand curve due to competition has been estimated).

20. Taylor (1994, 236–38) summarizes the size of the estimated network-externality effects. He concludes that the impact is quite small.

21. The elasticity for intrastate long-distance calls is significantly lower, but here I consider only interstate long-distance calls since the FCC regulates only those calls through its long-distance access charges.

22. This consistent elasticity finding is quite interesting given the real decrease in long-distance prices of about 50 percent over

this period as well as the outward shift of the demand curve, mainly due to increased incomes since the income elasticity of long-distance demand is about 1.0. (The consumer price index for interstate toll calls fell by approximately 25 percent from 1984 to 1994 so that real prices fell by more than 50 percent.)

23. In New York City, NYNEX (Bell Atlantic) offers only measured-rate local service.

24. The high inflation rates of the 1970s caused part of the increase in local access charges for residential service. As usual, regulators took a number of years before recognizing the increased costs of the inflationary period.

25. Local access and transport areas are geographically defined exchange areas that are generally formed around metropolitan areas. IntraLATA refers to calls that originate and terminate within a LATA.

26. Producer surplus is the difference between the selling price of a good and the cost to produce one more unit of that good. Consumer surplus is the difference between the price of a good and the price that the market is willing to pay for that good. At the margin, both these surpluses equal zero.

27. Even in a free-entry, imperfectly competitive industry with constant marginal cost and zero (economic) profits, price will exceed marginal cost.

28. Thus, as discussed above, I do not consider the possible distortions created by expenditure of the tax. I assume that all the quantities in the formulas are Hicksian compensated quantities. See Hausman (1981a) for computation of compensated quantities.

29. The $1.89 billion is the amount that I estimate will be raised from the tax on long-distance access; see footnote 12 for the calculation.

30. In general, no algebraic reason exists for the two estimates to be virtually identical as happens in the current situation.

31. Since the government institutions for the income tax are in place, the incremental administrative cost for the Internet subsidy would be extremely small. The federal universal service fund will finance a new government institution, the Universal Service Administrative Corporation, which will have significant fixed costs of operation. The FCC chose to establish this new administrative body, which will make the efficiency loss to the economy even greater than my calculations estimate it to be.

32. Of course, equity or distributional considerations also come into tax design. I discuss these considerations subsequently.

33. This estimate is for residential access. A one-standard-deviation change in the elasticity estimate would increase the mag-

nitude to –0.007 so that a very similar conclusion would follow. While I am unaware of similar estimates for business lines, I would expect the elasticity to be similar or even lower. Since 14.7 percent of households had second lines in 1995, however, the elasticity for these could well be higher. Given the higher income of residences with second lines, though, it is not necessarily the situation that the elasticity would be significantly higher. I am unaware of price elasticity estimates for these lines.

34. For residential second lines, the FCC did increase the SLC to $5.00 and indexed the rate to inflation. Second lines, however, are a low percentage of overall residential lines, since, as noted above, only about 14.7 percent of residences have second lines.

35. Numerous programs exist to subsidize telephone service for the needy. Besides a federal program, many states have their own programs. The details of the many programs and their overlap are too voluminous to be described here.

36. Since econometric estimates have not found a significant effect from network externalities—see, for example, Taylor (1994)—the $60,000 spent per household leads to almost no aggregate benefits.

37. AT&T promised the FCC that it would decrease its residential long-distance prices in 1997 when long-distance access prices decreased. Overall, the residential long-distance market has not been particularly competitive over the past five years.

38. From 1984 to 1990, the FCC regulated AT&T and generally required the firm to pass on decreases in long-distance access charges through lower long-distance prices.

39. Indeed, proponents of a Henry George approach to taxation should realize that the value of the electromagnetic spectrum could be an important addition to property-based taxation.

40. While long-distance users pay the SLC and per minute long-distance access charges, Internet users pay no fee because of an exemption granted by the FCC in 1988. Internet users have become a very powerful lobby through bulletin boards and e-mail to retain the subsidy they receive.

41. If, instead of the assumption that $\partial p_i / \partial t_i = 1$, I use a differentiated product oligopoly markup model assumption along with constant elasticity demand curves, the marginal efficiency loss could be higher than 1.25. Other oligopoly models, especially models based on linear demand curves, could find $\partial p_i / \partial t_i < 1$. Recent announcements by AT&T and MCI, however, state that long-distance rates will increase by 5.0 and 5.9 percent, respectively, to recover expenses incurred by the Telecommunications Act of 1996. This suggests that $\partial p / \partial t \approx 1$. It is interesting to note that despite quite large price

changes in long-distance service over the past twenty years, econometric estimates have found remarkably stable elasticity estimates. The second term in the right-side numerator of equation (C–1) may well decrease over time because of the increased SLC on second lines to residences and the per customer charges tax on long-distance companies. The decrease of the second term, however, is unlikely to offset increases in the first term in the numerator of equation (C–1) because of changes in technology. Furthermore, since the FCC intends to increase the tax revenue raised for universal service to almost $3 billion, this term may well increase initially, compared with changes that would have otherwise occurred, given the price-cap formula.

42. This assumption holds true since regulators set the price of local access.

43. Even if the first term in the right-side numerator of equation (D–1) were set to zero, the marginal efficiency effect of an increase in the SLC is more than 1,000 times smaller than the effect of the policy that the FCC actually chose.

# References

Auerbach, A. 1985. "The Theory of Excess Burden and Optimal Taxation." In A. Auerbach and M. Feldstein, *Handbook of Public Economics*, vol. 1. New York: North-Holland.

Ballard, C. L., J. B. Shoven, and J. Whalley. 1985. " General Equilibrium Computations of the Marginal Welfare Costs of Taxes in the United States." *American Economic Review* 75: 128–38.

Bouvenberg, A. L., and L. H. Goulder. 1996. "Optimal Environmental Taxation in the Presence of Other Taxes: General-Equilibrium Analyses." *American Economic Review* 86: 985–1000.

Browning, E. K. 1987. "On the Marginal Welfare Cost of Taxation." *American Economic Review* 77: 11–23.

Diamond, P., and J. Mirrlees. 1971. "Optimal Taxation and Public Production." *American Economic Review* 61: 8–27, 261–78.

Eriksson, R., D. Kaserman, and J. Mayo. 1995. "Targeted and Untargeted Subsidy Schemes: Evidence from Post-Divestiture Efforts to Promote Universal Telephone Service." Department of Economics, University of Tennessee, October.

Feldstein, M. 1995. "Tax Avoidance and the Deadweight Loss of the Income Tax." NBER working paper 5055.

Gatto, J., et al. 1988. "Interstate Switched Access Demand."
*Information Economics and Policy* 3.

Hausman, J. 1981a. "Exact Consumer's Surplus and Deadweight Loss." *American Economic Review* 71: 662–
76.

———. 1981b. "Income and Payroll Tax Policy and Labor
Supply." In L. Meyer, ed., *The Supply-Side Effects of
Economic Policy.* St. Louis: Federal Reserve Bank.

———. 1995. "Proliferation of Networks in Telecommunications: Technological and Economic Considerations."
In D. Alexander and W. Sichel, eds., *Networks, Infra-
structure, and the New Task for Regulation.* Ann Ar-
bor: University of Michigan Press.

———. 1997. "Valuation and the Effect of Regulation on
New Services in Telecommunications." *Brookings
Papers on Economic Activity: Microeconomics.*

Hausman, J., T. Tardiff, and A. Belinfante. 1993. "The Effects of the Breakup of AT&T on Telephone Penetration in the United States." *American Economic Review*
83 (2): 178–84.

Kahn, A. E. 1988. *The Economics of Regulation.* Cambridge, Mass.: MIT Press.

Laffont, J. J., and J. Tirole. 1996. "Competition in Telecommunications." Mimeo, November.

Perl, L. 1984. "A New Study of Economic and Demographic
Determinants of Residential Demand for Basic Tele-
phone Service." Mimeo, National Economic Research
Associates.

Posner, R. 1971. "Taxation by Regulation." *Bell Journal of
Economics and Management Science* 2: 22–50.

Poterba, J. 1997. "Do Budget Rules Work?" In A. Auerbach,
ed., *Fiscal Policy: Lessons from Economic Research.*
Cambridge, Mass.: MIT Press, pp. 53–86.

Solvason, D. 1997. "Cross-sectional Analysis of Residential Telephone Subscription in Canada Using 1994

Data." *Information Economics and Policy* 9: 241–64.

Taylor, L. 1994. *Telecommunications Demand in Theory and Practice*. Boston, Mass.: Kluwer Academic Publishers.

Taylor, W., and L. Taylor. 1993. "Postdivestiture Long-Distance Competition in the United States." *American Economic Review* 83: 185–90.

Temin, P. 1987. *The Fall of the Bell System*. Cambridge: Cambridge University Press.

# About the Author

JERRY HAUSMAN is MacDonald Professor of Economics at the Massachusetts Institute of Technology. He received the John Bates Clark Award of the American Economic Association in 1985 for the "most significant contributions to economics" for an economist under age forty. He also received the Frisch Medal from the Econometric Society in 1980. His research centers on econometrics, applied microeconomics, public finance, and telecommunications.